The Winds of Spirit Mountain

The Winds of Spirit Mountain
POEMS

Algirdas Zdanys

Grey Willow Press

Copyright © 2019 by Ramuté Zdanys Mills, Jonas Zdanys, and Leonas Zdanys. All rights reserved.

ISBN 978-1-7338882-1-9

Cover design by Regina Schroeder / forgetgutenberg.com

Acknowledgments
All except the last poem in this book were discovered neatly typed in a yellow folder labeled "Poetry" in the author's dresser after he died and are presented here in the order in which he left them. The last poem, which I have titled "Fragments from the Red Notebook," consists of fragments written, during his last months, in the red notebook he had by his side when he died. The fragments are presented here in the order in which they appear in his handwritten pages. JZ

Manufactured in the United States of America

Grey Willow Press
greywillowpress.org
greywillowpress@gmail.com

Contents

I Will If You Will
Poem
The Owl Calls
Brother of the Wind
The Old Trail of the Anasazi
The Smell of Stale Beer
Simple Lyrics of the Wind
PJC
The Littlest Bear
Simple Moments of Beauty
Their Home
Soft Sounds of Desert Winds
Overlooking Canyons
Chinde of the Anasazi
Memories in Shadows
Pictures in Memories
2
Endless Black Nights
Soft Black Velvet of Night
Moments in Time
Watching You Sleep
Memories of a Full Desert Moon
The Old Man
The Pond
52 Hours
At the Hands of Pain
An Old Man's Quest
Fragments from the Red Notebook

About the Author

I Will If You Will

They never talk even when they are talking.

They never listen even when they are listening.
I will
If you will, is what they hear.
I'll try if you try is what they say.
One waits for the other to try first.

In public they look good, they say all of the right
things.

They are like their friends, who live the same life,
the same lies.

The lies borne out of convenience, out of fear,
alcohol and drugs, make life bearable.
Each wondering why the other stays, but afraid to ask
the questions that need to be asked.
Failure is not an option, image and money is what
counts.

Love and self respect come last.

Their children are watching, learning from
the people they trust most.

I will if you will.

Poem

Ghost towns of the desert southwest,
surrounded by vast mountain ranges,
small cemeteries overlooking the
tumbleweed and broken windows,
once beautiful trees growing out of rooftops.
Soon the sun will rise above the
mountain ranges and unbearable
heat will settle into the nooks
and crannies of all that is left
of this town.
Through the branches of hundred
year old pine trees you can see
what's left of the mine openings,
dried up creek beds, fancy little
bridges missing the ornate wooden
etchings that once covered the sides.

The Owl Calls

Broken moonlight filters through the leaves as a solitary figure walks among a garden of stones.

A quiet desperation hangs over him.

The cold blue steel in his hand is telling him to behold the price of his journey.

He understands that time is short for midnight approaches and he hears the owl calling.

He stumbles and falls, he finds his past and his future.

He caresses the stone brushing away the twigs and dead leaves.

Tears cloud his eyes, he realizes that soon his heart will no longer ache.

He will be with her.

He never sees the flash nor smells the gunpowder.

The owl, startled for a moment, calls his name for the last time.

Brother of the Wind

I found him sitting at his favorite place under the tall ponderosa pines smoking his pipe, listening to the birds of the desert mountains singing their songs.

My old teacher looked tired, there was a sadness that hung heavy on his shoulders. We spent our time together talking about life, he told me he was tired of being alone, that his heart ached for his woman, he wanted to hear her voice, look into her eyes until she fell asleep, to smell her hair when she nuzzled into his chest, to laugh with her, to just hold her hand in his as they walked together.

I left my old teacher there, smoking his pipe, quietly singing the songs he had learned so long ago.

On a moonlit desert night, with the stars dancing across the sky, he crossed over to the other side where fields of yellow and orange flowers grew as far as the eyes could see, where the love of his life, the mother of his children, sat waiting for him under the branches of an old Joshua tree.

The Old Trail of the Anasazi

On this cold spring morning, I stand alone on
an old trail used by the Anasazi on their way
to Spirit Mountain,
flowers are beginning to sprout among patches
of snow and ice on the footworn trail.

A misty white cloud rolls down from the
snowcapped peak, through the mist, I watch
as a young maiden approaches, my heart
trembles.

Her dark hair dancing with the wind is hypnotic,
I am humbled by her beauty by her whispered
words of love.

With a strong gust of the North Wind the maiden
disappears back into the misty white cloud.

I am left alone with my eyes watering, the cold
north wind swirling along the old trail of the Anasazi.

The Smell of Stale Beer

Behind the walls of perfection there is an
emptiness in her life.

One day carries over to the next, days become
weeks, weeks become months and the years
roll by.

The emptiness that hangs so thick never seems
to leave, she finds it in every room, in every
corner, it even follows her in her car.

On most nights she wakes long before the
morning alarm, stairs creak ever so slightly
as she walks down to her favorite window
facing the southwestern sky.

She wonders how it could have been, tears gently
falling stain her chest.

The secrets in her life now will only live in her
memories.

As she walks from room to room the walls close
in around her squeezing the air from her chest.
The smell of stale beer lingers in the air gagging her.
Broken promises echoing from the den bounce their
way up the stairs forcing her to her knees.

She chooses to live in this world she knows so well, a world filled with fear and the smell of stale beer.

Simple Lyrics of the Wind

Last night I dreamt of a woman

    she was beautiful beyond words.

Her smile was like a blade of morning light that heats

the

      desert's cold.

   I looked into her eyes and saw hidden there the

     silence of forgotten things.

Thunder fell

    the rains came

I awoke and listened

    to the simple lyrics

of the wind.

PJC

He truly was larger than life, a bear of a man, with a gentleness of a child's heart, he was a son, a soldier, husband, father, grandfather and a friend.

He lived life according to his terms, doing more in his lifetime than most men would in two, he made, as he told it, many mistakes in his life, some large, some small, but he never hesitated to accept responsibility and he always stood tall.

He owned and flew planes and navigated rivers and ocean waters with boats that he owned, he owned businesses and real estate and had friends from all walks of life, he liked a glass of fine Scotch, foods of all kinds, he loved to laugh and always had a story to tell.

We became close these past few years, friends then brothers, one day we were laughing having lunch, talking about life, what he was looking forward to teaching his grandson, before he went on his final flight.

And then the next day he was gone.

We talk of him often at the gym, his second home, how you feel those penetrating moments of loneliness when you realize that he is gone.

That we will not hear his contagious laugh, see his eyes sparkling life whenever an interesting person walked by, as he was walking on his favorite treadmill or riding a bike. Nor see him nodding his head when he agreed with what you were saying, always adding "sure, sure sure."

But most of all when someone would say to him as they were leaving "see ya tomorrow Mr. C" and the response was always the same, "God Willing".

He was an important and vibrant part of so many lives and to so many creatures, he loved his country, his family, especially his grandson Gregory, and Kaz the cat.

He was a good man with a gentle soul, who loved to laugh, sometimes too loud, sometimes asked questions, better off not being asked, sometimes confessed his life's mistakes to too many people.

But that was just the way he was, a man who made mistakes and tried to make them right.

I do know this about him, he was loved by many and will be missed by many more.

The Littlest Bear

He stood by my side his trembling little hand holding
two of my fingers, that day he became my son.

We lived worlds apart but we listened to the same
wind, looked at the same stars, watched the sun set
deep into the western horizon, believed in the same
spirits and in the stories told by the old.

He taught me how to love without demands, how
to smile through pain,
how to speak without using words
how to listen with my eyes instead of my ears
how to touch anther person's heart when it was
filled with pain.

I think of him every day while sitting under tall
northern pines.
I can hear his laughter carried by the wind, feel the
warmth of his love in the rays of the setting sun.

I miss the littlest bear and I wait for the day when
we can run together chasing after the wind.

Simple Moments of Beauty

No matter what has happened in her life she has always kept her heart, she understands her place in a world filled with pain, sadness and mistrust.

She has learned to seek simple moments of beauty that give her joy:
the flowers that she nurtures in her gardens give her a sense of accomplishment,
her trips throughout the years to the waters of her youth that hold so many memories,
the loss of her innocence becoming a woman with all the passions that she still holds dear.

Watching her children grow and leave their nest to build lives of their own, her memories will sustain her when her heart aches for the hugs that they gave her, when she made it all better.

Their Home

She watches her children sleep
waiting for the first rays of
sunlight to transform their quiet
home.

This is her favorite time of day
waiting for the stillness of her
home to go away.

Waiting for her children to wake
and rub the sleep away.

Sitting together having breakfast
enjoying a simple moment.

Planning their day.

This is what his life was meant for
waiting for the stillness to go away.

Soft Sounds of Desert Winds

I would find him standing alone on a desert path
in the high mountain country,
his jet black eyes looking off into distant horizons,
he told me he was watching those who went on
their final journeys before him, dancing with hawks
and eagles on stages of rolling white clouds.

He would smile when he saw clouds shaped like
animals float by as warm desert breezes brushed
his hair from his eyes.

I would sit with him for hours watching the sun set
behind canyon walls,
the sun's reflections casting red and orange flames
in his jet black eyes as we listened to the soft sounds
of desert winds go by.

Overlooking Canyons

I carried the littlest bear on my shoulders as we walked to our favorite spot overlooking canyons.

His chin resting on top of my head he started to cry, his tears touching my heart as they fell from his snowy white cheeks.

He seldom cried but the painful events of the day brought the tears.

He squeezed my neck a little harder, his jet black eyes shining like two buttons on a snowman's face, as we searched the far horizons for a shooting star.

Hoping to make a wish.

Chinde of the Anasazi

He sits alone in the prehistoric kitchen, where the
campfires of the Anasazi Warriors once burnt bright
and warmed the cold winter nights of long ago.

He has come a long way seeking a better
understanding of life, hoping to learn the old ways.

He feels the presence of the Chinde all around him,
as they reach out and touch his spirit, brush up against
him, they are drawn to the warmth of his heart, the
honesty in his eyes.

But are confused by the pain in his spirit, the sadness
that hangs over his head.

The Chinde call out to the heavens that surround the
canyon, calling on Golden Eagle to come and drop
a feather, so that it would float down from the heavens
and land between them.

So they could talk honestly from their hearts, learn the
secrets that live in this man, that make his heart heavy.

So they sit waiting, hoping, for Golden Eagle to come
soon and drop a feather.
Time is short they hear the owl calling his name.

Memories in Shadows

The oldman remembers as he walks the dark streets of
his youth, searching for yesterdays
afraid of tomorrows,
seeking simplicity to his life.

Shadows of those who lived there greet him from
behind hedges and trees as he walks by,
he hears their voices
sees their faces in memories.

In his youth the oldman found comfort hiding
in shadows,
especially when he was afraid or made mistakes,
hoping that no one would see,
but someone always did.

Now as an oldman he pays a price for hiding in the
shadows of his youth.

Fear and indecision guide his life.

He has traveled many miles been to many places, gone
down many roads, hoping to rid his life of fear and
indecision, but they are his constant companions.

So the oldman returns to the shadows and memories of
his youth.

Hoping he will learn something to regain control of his life.

To live his life free of indecision and fear.

Pictures in Memories

I hold her picture in my heart and in my memories.

There it will never grow old nor fade.

I will be able to see her soft eyes the delicate features of her face.

Feel the passions of her heart anytime I want.

I will be able to love her forever, never worry about who is watching, a reconciliation, or another change of heart.

The sun set and the full moon hung high over the desert, you stood wrapped in a soft white robe, looking out the window.

Your face bathed in moonlight was more beautiful than any portraits painted by the great masters.

Michelangelo, Rembrandt, Degas, and da Vinci they all would have been humbled by your beauty,

a beauty that comes from the very depths of your soul.

The light from the full moon has long since faded into the western horizon.

I sit alone in the darkness of my room, with memories and the faint smell of your perfume.

I miss

I will always love you.

Bear

Endless Black Nights

Tears falling from her cheeks stain the hardwood floors.

Looking out the window, she sees the first light of dawn break through the blackness of this late winter's night.

She has seen this many times before.

There is no escape for her, she is trapped in a life she knows so well.

A life she lives by choice, out of fear of what others might say or think.

When she is alone she curls up in the shower hoping to relive memories that hang in the steamy mist covering the bathroom glass.

Water bouncing off of her skin mixes with her tears.

Without any doubt the memories in her heart will be locked away forever.

There is nothing left for her to do but live her life and become one with the endless black nights of late winter days.

Soft Black Velvet of Night

As I walk through the darkness looking for you
I hear you softly call out.

I find you in the den lying in front of a crackling fire,
as you reach out to me, shadows dance on the
ceiling, it feels good to be held by you,
to feel the softness of your breasts the warmth of
your body.

I never want it to end.

A storm rages outside, the wind is howling, a clap
of thunder shakes me to the bone.

I reach out for you but you are not there.

The fire had died out a chill had settled in, I was
left alone with memories of a dream so real.

I could hear the muffled rumble of distant thunder
as the soft black velvet of night returned.

I closed my eyes hoping to sleep.

To dream.

Moments in Time

Fingers barely touching eyes avoiding contact humid air covering our skin. As the wind scatters our thoughts throughout the pale blue sky.

Our lives will not change for we have learned that from the seeds of small lies grow small truths.

I promised you that my love would never die, but it will wait for the moment in time when our fingers touch our eyes lock and our hearts beat as one.

Watching You Sleep

You fell asleep as I held you in my arms, I gently kissed your lips.

You smiled oh so gently as you drifted deeper into the land of dreams.

Your skin glowed like the soft stars glittering in the black desert sky.

As I watched you sleep, I saw in your face the innocence of youth.

I fell deeper in love with you, never thinking that it was possible to love you more than I already did.

The light of the desert moon reached out and touched both of our hearts, as you nuzzled closer into my arms and stole what was left of my heart.

Memories of a Full Desert Moon

You left hours ago and I still feel your presence in the room, the soft scent of citrus lingers gently.

I close my eyes and I am lying next to you, watching you sleep, listening to the soft sounds of your breathing, watching your chest rise and fall with each deep breath.

To me you are as beautiful as a single white rose in a field of red roses.

My mind drifts back to the last night we spent together, when you took my hand in yours and gently pulled me down next to you.

You caressed my face and touched my lips ever so softly.

I could not take my eyes off of you, we kissed passionately, we kissed again and again, you opened your heart and let me walk in.

You put your head on my chest and we lie quietly listening to our hearts beating as one.

The Old Man

The old man with soft blue eyes and weatherbeaten
skin sits slowly rocking, looking down the old
mountain path, his eyes filled with hope.

An empty rocking chair next to his slowly rocks in the
wind, I see him beckoning me to join him, the old chair
creaks as I lower myself into it, waiting for the old man
to tell his story about the only woman he ever loved,
his quivering voice touching my heart every time.

I watch shadows dance on the faces of rocks smoothed
by time as he and his words are carried by the wind
to far corners of distant mountain passes.

So here on the porch of his little cabin at the top
of Bear Mountain, the old man waits, slowly rocking,
looking down the old mountain path lined
with wildflowers, waiting for her to come and sit
awhile, so they could hold hands and listen to the wind
as they slowly rock and time passes by.

A crack of thunder startles me,
opening my eyes I see the reflection of the old man
shimmering in a puddle, his weatherbeaten face
filled with loneliness, his soft blue eyes looking
helplessly down the old mountain path.

My eyes fill with tears as I sit slowly rocking, listening to the wind as an empty old rocking chair next to mine slowly rocks in the wind.

The Pond

Water lapping onto the rocky shore just inches
from our dangling toes makes you giggle.

A sole leaf with all the colors of fall
splashed onto its curling skin slowly floats by.

Arms wrapped around each other, passions
building as the sun warms the cool fall air.

Our time together is short,
circumstances make it so.

So we sit exchanging hurried kisses,
quick hidden caresses, soft sighs.

I am happy with whatever time you can give
on this cool fall day,

as we watch the leaf slowly drift away.

52 Hours

On this cold desert night I waited for time to stop.

It did not.

I wanted to go back 52 hours to be able to see her eyes full of happiness when she saw me standing by the arrival gate, to walk arm in arm bodies pressed close.

To watch her sleep with the blue desert moon shining through the window.

But this could not be so we waited for the sadness to end for the laughter to return, but it did not.

I felt her heart break as her tears found their way down her soft cheeks.

I closed my eyes trying to squeeze back the tears, to breathe without pain, to pretend that this was all a dream, that the sound of laughter would return.

But it did not.

I watched the door slowly close behind her trying to find comfort in the blackness of the room, losing track of time waiting for the door to burst open, to hear

Hi honey I'm home.

At the Hands of Pain

Because of the order of her birth, her
lot in life,
she sought out attention of anyone who
showed that they might care,
she needed to be the bright star even for
a moment,
even at the hands of pain she gladly accepted,
so she sought out attention never realizing
it was all in vain.

She did not understand the meaning of her life.

One day while walking through a meadow not
far from where she was raised,
she saw a light where the meadow met a forest path,
as she drew near the light guided her to the
moss laden path and beckoned her to follow.

As she walked among the tall pines,
white birches, tall oak trees she grew at peace,
she realized that who she is did not come from
what she did, or what she had, her power came
from the paths she chose to travel none of them
ever being the same.

An Old Man's Quest

I walk among rocks shaped like animals carved
by the desert winds of the southwest.

My spirit is young but for some reason I have the
body of an old man.

I have been told that there are gentle spirits that
live in these desert mountains that have the answers
to all of life's questions.

Answers that I seek to questions that I need to ask,
but all I hear is laughter in the wind.
As it rattles its way through my head, making it
impossible to choose my words, decide what
directions to take.

I am running out of time to find the answers I seek to
questions about my irrelevant past and my uncertain
future.

All I keep hearing is laughter in the wind as it rattles
its way through my head on its way to far mountain
passes.

Fragments from the Red Notebook

*

I need to be seen
Somebody please I am
alone

*

I find I am a man and
more affected by the violent
deaths of people I grew up with since
kindergarten

*

Heather
age
Nos of years in Police work 33yr
Working years with State Police 21 yr
Working until next promotion ----
Classes of certifications
Any class of certifications she might
have that would be healthful
Anything that would be healthful?
Healthy relationships with PS expounding

vs within two cities over
Should there be any Sargeant Indices. Yes
Weaking links
Who would control the equipment
from the patrol cars to what's in them.
Major.
Should there be an appointed honor guard
or should there be a year.

*

Attic to ground floor outside.
6 ft ramp
ramp
6 ft ramp
10 ft wall
attic storage
attic cutout
attic storage.

*

Glass tile + Cinder Block
to side greenhouses
North
South
West
East
Corner Glass Greenhouse
Fireplace

or
Grill to
bring Heat
Glass House

*

Glass Blocks
2 inch ramp
Brick/Cinder
Block Building
air Vent on the
Roof
Rearwall
No windows studs cones

*

No.

3.
4.

*

Island Requirements.

Choices:
1ˢᵗ Island off the coast of Northern California
1.50 – 2.00 miles in size

2ⁿᵈ Island
¾ mile to little over 1 mile.
¼ of a mile to ¾ to 1 mile.

3ʳᵈ Island
One of the islands with the Great Lakes
size about accessibility

4ᵗʰ Island off the coast of Maine

5ᵗʰ Island off the coast of New England,
New Jersey, New York, Rhode Island, Connecticut,
Maryland, Maine, Greenland, Iceland

? Island off the coast of

*

K – 12   8
                    Table 10
                                9

*

Bottom

        Back

        Front

Wall

*

Weapons

1   Short cleaning supplies
2   Bullets

*

Bear (vs) Evil

Evil:
(1) 3 to 4 minutes per round if things are going good for the opponent
(2) 4 – 5 minutes in between rounds if things are going good for the Evil Team
(3) The bell stops the fight
(4) Fight doctor can stop the Round and the Fight
(5) Referee or the doctor can stop all fight shenanigans and the Fight itself
(6) Referee can stop the fight for any illegal Substance or Article of Clothing

Includes metal brass knuckles and
volumes of chain

BEAR CHOICE
(1) Whatever illegal things
Evil tries to bring
into the ring
Bear will determine which
things are illegal by agreement
with the Referee

(2) Nevada and the WB Associations
which control what can be placed on
the Fighters.

If I die the Money my share
will be divided with Evil.

(3) If I Die I
will be cremated
and my ashes will be divided
to all my children
given by marriage.

49 percent to the Winner.
49 % of the Money
given to the Association
to bring dead back.

That should leave me
5 Dollars give or take

4 Dollars.

I would like to say
I have always loved
my children
I buried all the ones that
died.

That's it.......

*

I especially love
StaLy and he children—
None of which were
mine/

I loved many vimmens –
none of whose were my
wife.

I forgive any she might
after me.
And I will all love
her.

I hope she goes to the
after funeral snack
bar.

Say I loved all my 9
old girl friends
even after they brought me
back.

and I died
5— to ten months
Later.

* * * * * * * * * *

I love my Family
Forever.
and all my daughters
and sons who didn't
uses protections.

* * * * * * * * * *

About the Author

Algirdas Zdanys was born in New Britain, Connecticut, on November 23, 1953, and died on November 17, 2018. He grew up in New Britain, attended New Britain schools, and earned a bachelor's degree in sociology from Central Connecticut State University. He put his many talents and skills with people to work as a policeman in Newington, Connecticut, where he served for many years, and then, after retiring, as a private investigator with his own detective agency. He was an avid photographer, a poet, a storyteller, and a humorist who kept all who knew him happy and entertained. But above all he was Uncle Owl to his nieces and nephews, whom he loved and cherished every day, and for many of whom he was a loving and active godfather, a special position in the family that he celebrated with great joy. And, he was Al (and sometimes Bear) to his many friends, throughout the country and in the Navajo nation, whose friendships he valued and to whose aid he would come readily with a smile and a steady hand.

www.ingramcontent.com/pod-product-compliance
Lightning Source LLC
Chambersburg PA
CBHW060507080526
44584CB00015B/1590